CURIOSITY'S MISSION ON MARS

EXPLORING THE RED PLANET

TWENTY-FIRST CENTURY BOOKS / MINNEAPOLIS

CURIOSITY'S MiSSiON ON MarS

EXPLORING THE RED PLANET

RON MiLLEr

TWENTY-FIRST CENTURY BOOKS / MiNNEAPOLIS

This book is dedicated to Georgia Eli Browning,
who may someday leave her footprints on Mars.
—RM

Twenty-First Century Books
A division of Lerner Publishing Group, Inc.
241 First Avenue North
Minneapolis, MN 55401 USA

For reading levels and more information, look up this title at www.lernerbooks.com.

Main body text set in Univers LT Std. 11/15. Typeface provided by Adobe Systems.

Library of Congress Cataloging-in-Publication Data

Miller, Ron, 1947– author.
    Curiosity's mission on Mars: Exploring the red planet/ by Ron Miller.
        pages   cm
    Includes bibliographical references and index.
    ISBN 978–1–4677–1087–9 (lib. bdg. : alk. paper)
    ISBN 978–1–4677–2547–7 (ebook)
    1. Mars (Planet)—Juvenile literature. 2. Mars (Planet)—Exploration—Juvenile
literature. I. Title.
QB641.M539 2014
523.43—dc23   2013009290

Manufactured in the United States of America
1 – PC – 12/31/13

CONTENTS

NASA's Mars Science Laboratory mission clears the tower at Cape Canaveral Air Force Station in Florida at 10:02 a.m. (Eastern Standard Time) on November 26, 2011. The mission will spend at least one Martian year (687 days) on the red planet.

CHAPTER 1

a STRANGE VISITOR - - - - ⌐

Life on Mars? In May 2013 the space rover *Curiosity* discovered evidence of ancient streambeds on the red planet where rivers would have flowed millions of years ago. And in late September 2013, *Curiosity* made another discovery scientists had been waiting for. It found that 2 percent of the surface of Mars consists of water. This is equivalent to two pints (0.9 liters) of water in every cubic foot (0.03 cubic meters) of Martian soil. If there is this much water on Mars today, there must have been vast quantities—seas, rivers, and lakes—on Mars millions of years ago.

Learning more about water on ancient and present-day Mars is one of the key goals of the Mars Science Laboratory (MSL) mission. With this evidence—along with Martian rock samples showing the existence of key chemicals for life—scientists have added more proof to the theory that Mars could once have sustained life of some kind. It also increases the possibility that humans may one day be able to live on the red planet. These dramatic discoveries were set into motion on November 26, 2011, when a rocket launched by the US National Aeronautics and Space Administration (NASA) took off from Earth. The rocket was carrying one of the most complex machines—the *Curiosity* rover—ever to be launched into space. On August 5, 2012—254 days after launching from Cape Canaveral Air Force Station in Florida—the

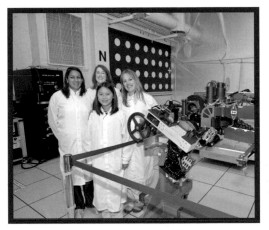

NAMING *CURIOSITY*

Three years before the launch of the MSL mission, NASA held a student contest to name the rover. Every entry had to be accompanied by an essay explaining the student's suggestion. Clara Ma *(at right, in front)*, a sixth-grade student in Kansas, won the contest. In her essay, Clara wrote, "Curiosity is an everlasting flame that burns in everyone's mind. It makes me get out of bed in the morning and wonder what surprises life will throw at me that day. Curiosity is such a powerful force. Without it, we wouldn't be who we are today. Curiosity is the passion that drives us through our everyday lives. We have become explorers and scientists with our need to ask questions and to wonder."

After Clara won the contest, NASA invited her to the headquarters of the Jet Propulsion Lab (JPL) in Pasadena, California. JPL is NASA's center for the robotic exploration of space. It is in charge of the MSL mission. At JPL Clara signed her name on the rover. She was also invited to Florida for the launch.

Clara observed that "I thought space was something I could only read about in books and look at during the night from so far away. I thought that I would never be able to get close to it, so for me, naming the Mars rover would at least be one step closer."

spacecraft reached the red planet. The MSL rover it carried is larger and heavier than previous models. The size of a small SUV, the rover weighs 1,982 pounds (899 kilograms) and stands 7 feet (2.2 meters) tall.

LANDING THE ROVER

Engineers knew the landing of such a mammoth craft would be tricky, so they invented a completely new way of landing that did not rely on previous airbag systems and legged landers. The unmanned MSL spacecraft consists of two parts: a computer-controlled module known as a descent stage and the *Curiosity* rover attached to the bottom. The descent stage had a rocket at each of its four corners and a radar system for relaying information about the rover's altitude and velocity.

When the MSL spacecraft reached Mars, it was traveling at a speed of 13,000 miles (21,000 kilometers) per hour. At such speed, scientists know, a spacecraft will burn up from the heat created by friction within Mars's atmosphere. So they installed the largest high-tech heat shield—15 feet (4.5 m) in diameter—ever to travel to another planet.

FRICTION

Friction causes heat. You can easily discover this by rubbing the palms of your hands together. As you do so, your palms quickly grow warm. The same thing happens when a meteoroid enters the atmosphere of a planet. The air rushing past the meteoroid rubs against it and makes it grow warmer. If the meteoroid is going fast enough, it will grow hot enough to glow brightly. It may even get hot enough to burn up entirely.

At night, you might see a bright streak of light in the sky. Some people call these streaks shooting stars, but they are actually meteoroids burning up high in Earth's atmosphere. When a meteoroid grows hot enough to be visible, it is called a meteor.

The same thing happens to a spacecraft entering the atmosphere of a planet. So scientists take precautions to prevent the spacecraft from burning up. One of the precautions is to equip a spacecraft with heat shields. Made of materials that carry heat away from the spacecraft, the shields slow the spacecraft to speeds that generate safer levels of friction and heat.

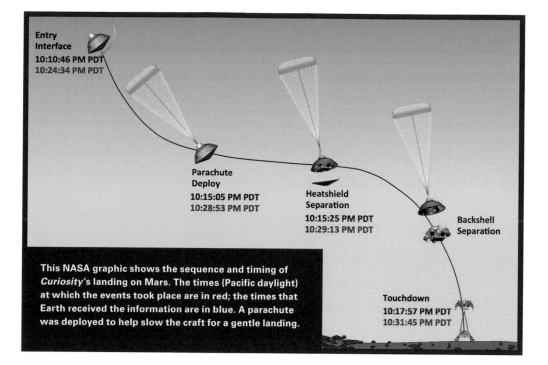

Entry
Interface
10:10:46 PM PDT
10:24:34 PM PDT

Parachute
Deploy
10:15:05 PM PDT
10:28:53 PM PDT

Heatshield
Separation
10:15:25 PM PDT
10:29:13 PM PDT

Backshell
Separation

Touchdown
10:17:57 PM PDT
10:31:45 PM PDT

This NASA graphic shows the sequence and timing of *Curiosity*'s landing on Mars. The times (Pacific daylight) at which the events took place are in red; the times that Earth received the information are in blue. A parachute was deployed to help slow the craft for a gentle landing.

To prepare for landing, the descent stage rockets slowed down the craft to about 1,000 miles (1,610 km) per hour, and the landing system triggered the release of a parachute to slow the spacecraft even further. When the craft had slowed to about 360 miles (580 km) per hour, the spacecraft's computer jettisoned (released into space) the heat shield. At a speed of 223 miles (160 km) per hour and at an altitude of just over 1 mile (1.8 km), the parachute was disconnected and allowed to float away. The four rocket engines of the landing system then began firing. The thrust of the engines slowed *Curiosity*'s descent even further. At this time, the rover's wheels were deployed. The computer ordered the sky-crane landing system to lower the rover with 25-foot (7.6 m) cables onto the surface of Mars at Gale Crater, near the Martian equator. When the rover's sensors detected touchdown, the descent stage took off at full speed, crashing at a safe distance from the rover.

The mission's landing site had been very carefully chosen. Gale Crater is 96 miles (154 km) in diameter. It is larger than the states of Rhode Island and Delaware combined. In the middle is Mount Sharp, a mountain about 3 miles (5 km) high. Near the foot of the mountain are claylike minerals. Above these are layers with minerals containing sulfur and oxygen. All of these layers contain elements vital to life.

BRADBURY LANDING

The MSL mission landing site is named Bradbury Landing to honor science fiction author Ray Bradbury *(right)*, who died on June 5, 2012, just two months before the spacecraft landed. The naming took place on August 22, 2012, which would have been the author's ninety-second birthday. In the 1950s, Bradbury wrote *The Martian Chronicles,* a collection of short stories about human colonization of the red planet.

MISSIONS TO MARS

Ever since NASA's first attempt to reach Mars in 1960, more than forty American, Russian, and European spacecraft have been launched toward the red planet. Only seventeen made it. Some of these barely left the ground, some failed along the way, and others crashed into the planet. So many spacecraft have been lost trying to reach Mars that a magazine reporter jokingly suggested that a space monster must be eating them. He called the fictional monster the "Great Galactic Ghoul."

Almost all of the Mars missions have had similar goals, primarily to detect signs of water and other key elements of life. Among the most successful NASA spacecraft to reach Mars was *Mariner 4,* which flew past the planet on July 14, 1965. It was followed by *Mariner 6* and *Mariner 7. (Mariner 5* was a mission to Venus.) These provided the first close-up photographs of the planet, revealing Mars to have craters, giant volcanoes, and huge valleys.

In July 1976, the *Viking 1* and *Viking 2* spacecraft arrived on Mars—the first to land on the planet. Each spacecraft consisted of a lander and an orbiter. The landers sent back photos and information about the landscape from the Martian surface. The orbiters circled the planet, taking additional pictures from space. One of the main goals of the *Viking* landers was to look for signs of life on Mars. Scientists are still arguing over the results. Some say that no signs of life were found, while more recent evaluation of the *Viking* data suggests evidence for microbial life on Mars. The orbiters did make an important discovery. Their images show evidence of erosion and of deep valleys and channels characteristic of the effects of giant floods of water. Evidence of branched streams in other parts of Mars suggests that rain might once have fallen there.

The *Pathfinder* spacecraft carried the first rover—*Sojourner*—to land on Mars. The 23-pound (10.6 kg), toaster-sized *Sojourner* made important measurements in 1997, but its real mission was to serve as a test run for future, larger rovers.

The *Mars Global Surveyor* arrived in 1997. Its goal was to explore Mars from orbit. Over the next several years, it studied the Martian surface and atmosphere, revealing additional evidence of water on Mars. This water is not on the surface in lakes and rivers, however, but is deep underground.

Spacecraft engineers with three generations of Mars rovers developed by the Jet Propulsion Lab in Pasadena, California. The rovers include a flight spare for *Sojourner (front)* from 1997; a test rover resembling *Spirit* and *Opportunity (left)* that dates to the early 2000s; and a test rover *(right)* that served as a model for *Curiosity*.

In the early 2000s, two more spacecraft reached Mars. In 2001 NASA's *Mars Odyssey* orbiter discovered signs of hydrogen at the planet's south pole. The large amounts of hydrogen are signs of huge quantities of water ice beneath the surface surrounding the south pole. Water is made mostly of hydrogen, a very light gas. When water breaks down in the presence of some minerals, this gas escapes and is easy to detect.

In 2003 the European Space Agency (ESA) launched the *Mars Express* orbiter and a lander called *Beagle 2*. The lander failed, but the orbiter took detailed photos of the surface of Mars. It too discovered the presence of water ice at the planet's south pole.

After landing on Mars in 2004, NASA's *Spirit* and *Opportunity* rovers were meant to operate on Mars for only 92 days and to travel about 0.75 miles (1 km) on the Martian surface. Instead, after more than eight years and 20 miles (32 km), *Opportunity* is still busy exploring. *Spirit* finally ran out of power in 2010. Both rovers sent back close-up photos of the Martian surface and, like other missions, discovered evidence that the planet was once covered with water.

UNDERGROUND ICE

If Mars once had so much water, where did it go? Though most of the missing water was probably lost to evaporation, *Curiosity* discovered that a lot of water is bound up in the Martian soil. But scientists believe that most of the water remaining on Mars may exist in the form of underground ice, lying not far beneath the surface of Mars. This would be similar to the permafrost (a permanent layer of ice) that lies beneath Earth's tundra landscapes.

In 2002 the *Mars Global Surveyor* spacecraft detected signs of hydrogen atoms that suggest the presence of what may be a vast ocean of underground ice on Mars. At the equator, for instance, the top of the ice layer on Mars may be between 1,000 and 3,000 feet (300 m and 1 km)

This image, taken by a camera on the Mars Reconnaissance Orbiter in 2008, shows wandering and braided patterns typical of channels carved by water.

beneath the surface, where the ice may be as thick as 0.6 to 1.9 miles (1 to 3 km). At higher latitudes it may be only 500 to 1,000 feet (150 to 300 m) beneath the surface and 1.9 to 4.3 miles (3 to 7 km) thick.

Images from NASA's Mars Reconnaissance Orbiter have also revealed channels or gullies that may be evidence of groundwater seeping from the slopes of craters and valleys in the southern hemisphere of Mars. Since the channels appear on top of sand dunes, the channels must have been created more recently than the dunes themselves. It is possible that the dunes are millions of years old, but if the channels are in an area where dunes are constantly changing and being recreated, the water deposits may be very young.

Some scientists have concluded that water is still flowing on Mars. This would be possible if the Martian water is brine—water with high concentrations of dissolved mineral salts. Brine does not evaporate as quickly as water alone.

One of the most successful missions to Mars has been NASA's Mars Reconnaissance Orbiter, which arrived in 2006. Its high-powered cameras have sent back amazingly detailed photos of the Martian surface, while its instruments have measured water, ice, and minerals on and beneath the surface.

NASA's *Phoenix* lander set down near the north pole of Mars in 2008. Like previous missions, an important goal was to look for signs of water on the planet. *Phoenix's* robotic arm dug trenches in the soil surrounding the lander. It discovered water ice only inches beneath the surface.

MOVING AROUND

In comparison to previous craft, *Curiosity* is a high-tech wonder. It is not only the largest rover to land on Mars, but also the most complex. It even has its own computer brain so it can function without a human driver. This is important because Mars is so far away from Earth. Depending on where each planet is in its orbit, the two can be as far away as 250 million miles (401 million km) from each other. Even when the two planets are nearest one another, it takes light three minutes to travel from Mars to Earth.

When the rover landed, Mars was 154 million miles (248 million km) from our planet. At that distance, the first signals took fourteen minutes to reach Earth. It took another fourteen minutes for a reply from Earth to arrive back on Mars. As *Curiosity* moves around on the surface of Mars, a lot can happen in that timeframe. For instance, it could fall off a cliff long before scientists back on Earth would even know about it. For this reason, the rover needs to be able to make some decisions on its own.

The rover sits on six aluminum wheels. Each wheel has its own electric motor. The two front and two rear wheels each have individual steering motors. These allow *Curiosity* to spin in a full 360-degree circle. Four-wheel steering also allows *Curiosity* to make very tight turns so it can easily avoid obstacles.

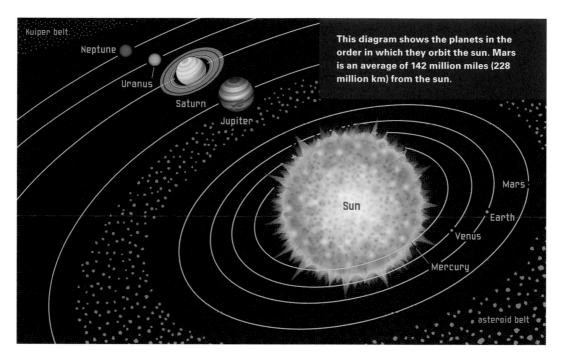

This diagram shows the planets in the order in which they orbit the sun. Mars is an average of 142 million miles (228 million km) from the sun.

CAMERAS AT WORK

To help it make decisions, the MSL rover is equipped with ten cameras (with a total of seventeen lenses) that function as its eyes. Some of these help the rover steer and look at rock and soil specimens. Other cameras give a full-color, 3-D view of the landscape around the rover. These 3-D cameras are on the top of a mast that raises them about 6 feet (1.8 m) above the ground. The cameras relay the view to NASA scientists on Earth. The view is similar to what an adult would see if standing on the surface of Mars. These cameras can also take color video, and they have powerful zoom lenses.

The remaining cameras help with navigation and sample analysis. Four Hazard Avoidance Cameras (Hazcams) are mounted underneath the rover, at the front and back. These help prevent the rover from getting lost or accidentally running into something. Two other navigation cameras—called Navcams—are mounted on the mast with the color 3-D cameras. These also help the rover navigate on its own. All of the cameras are connected to the rover's computer brain so it can make its own decisions about how to safely navigate the Martian landscape.

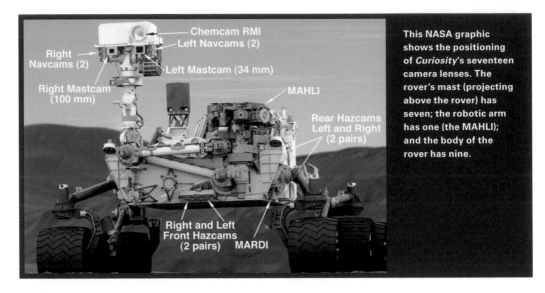

Chemcam RMI
Left Navcams (2)
Right Navcams (2)
Left Mastcam (34 mm)
Right Mastcam (100 mm)
MAHLI
Rear Hazcams Left and Right (2 pairs)
Right and Left Front Hazcams (2 pairs)
MARDI

This NASA graphic shows the positioning of *Curiosity*'s seventeen camera lenses. The rover's mast (projecting above the rover) has seven; the robotic arm has one (the MAHLI); and the body of the rover has nine.

TOOLS FOR EXPLORATION

To carry out its mission, *Curiosity* is equipped with a wide range of high-tech tools. For example, the rover has a robotic arm and hand that can be controlled by an operator on Earth. With five joints, the arm is very flexible. It is equipped with a hand that can reach and examine rocks and other objects. NASA scientists are using the arm and the rover's other tools to investigate samples in the quest to find key elements of life.

Alpha Particle X–Ray Spectrometer (APXS)

One of the rover's tools is a spectrometer that allows the rover to determine the different kinds and amounts of chemical elements in the rock and soil of Mars. Knowing what elements make up Martian rocks provides scientists with information about how the surface of Mars was formed. The spectrometer uses alpha particles and X-rays to take images of the Martian landscape. Scientists know that alpha particles are emitted during the decay of radioactive materials. X-rays are a type of electromagnetic radiation, like light and microwaves. The APXS shoots beams of X-rays and helium nuclei at Martian rocks and records the X-ray radiation that bounces back. Depending on the chemical elements in the rock, the radiation waves will present a unique pattern. By looking at these patterns, NASA scientists can determine what elements are in the sample.

Curiosity's Navcam took this image of the rover's robotic arm touching a rock on the Martian surface in September 2012. The rover's APXS instrument assessed the chemical makeup of the rock, which scientists named Jake Matijevic in honor of Jacob Matijevic, a Mars rover engineer who died in 2012.

Mars Hand Lens Imager (MAHLI)

This imager is one of the rover's many cameras. It works just like the magnifying glass a geologist might use to examine a mineral specimen. It provides scientists with highly detailed views of the structure of rocks and soil on Mars. The MAHLI's camera takes color images of features smaller than the diameter of a human hair.

Rock Abrasion Tool

The rock abrasion tool is a powerful grinder. It can create a hole in a rock about 2 inches (51 mm) wide and 0.2 inches (5 mm) deep. This tool is important because the inside of a rock can be very different from its surface. Being able to examine the inside of a rock can help scientists understand how the rock was formed and the kinds of environmental conditions that changed it. When scientists analyzed the first samples of Martian dust gathered by the tool, they discovered that the dust contained some of the key chemical ingredients necessary for life, such as carbon, hydrogen, oxygen, nitrogen, sulfur, and phosphorus.

Miniature Thermal Emission Spectrometer (Mini-TES)

The Mini-TES is another instrument designed to discover the makeup of Martian soil and rocks. It can do this from a distance by detecting and measuring the heat they emit. Individual objects emit heat

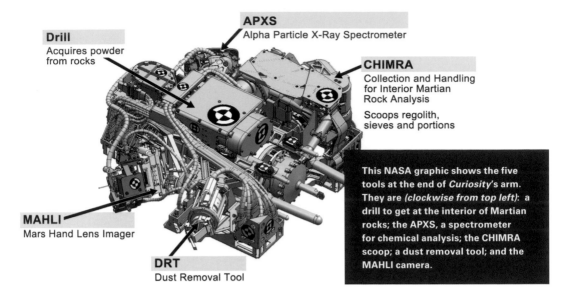

Drill
Acquires powder
from rocks

APXS
Alpha Particle X-Ray Spectrometer

CHIMRA
Collection and Handling
for Interior Martian
Rock Analysis

Scoops regolith,
sieves and portions

MAHLI
Mars Hand Lens Imager

DRT
Dust Removal Tool

This NASA graphic shows the five
tools at the end of *Curiosity*'s arm.
They are *(clockwise from top left)*: a
drill to get at the interior of Martian
rocks; the APXS, a spectrometer
for chemical analysis; the CHIMRA
scoop; a dust removal tool; and the
MAHLI camera.

differently. These differences can help scientists identify the minerals
and other elements on Mars.

Mössbauer Spectrometer

This spectrometer is designed to look for minerals that are rich in iron.
Several magnets, which naturally detect iron, are located on different
places on the rover. They are used to separate magnetic materials
from samples of Martian dust. Magnetic particles carry important
clues about water because many magnetic minerals form only in the
presence of water.

Many of the erosion features that have been seen on Mars, such
as channels, could possibly have been made by wind or dry ice—and
not water. So scientists are looking for more evidence that water once
flowed on the surface of the planet. And if water was once abundant
on Mars, they want to know where it went.

Sample Analysis at Mars (SAM) and Chemistry and Mineralogy (CheMin)

In early December 2012, *Curiosity* began using its built-in laboratory
to test the Martian soil. The laboratory is called the Sample Analysis
at Mars, or SAM. It also uses a tool called the Chemistry and

Mineralogy, or CheMin. The SAM heats a soil sample until it gives off gases. It then uses a spectroscope to identify the elements that make up the gases. The CheMin uses X-rays to examine specimens gathered by the rover's tools.

In the samples, scientists discovered sulfur, chlorine, and hints of carbon. Carbon is one of the building blocks of organic compounds. But finding carbon is not the same as finding life. "Just finding carbon somewhere doesn't mean that it has anything to do with life or the finding of a habitable environment," says lead *Curiosity* scientist and mission spokesperson John Grotzinger.

SAM was instrumental in discovering that another important ingredient for life—water—exists on Mars in great quantities. It did this by passing hot helium gas over a sample of Martian soil. Its spectroscope detected the different gases that were released. Among these were large quantities water vapor. Also released, however, were chemicals called perchlorates. These are poisonous, and if too much of these chemicals exists on Mars, it might be a problem for future human settlers.

POWER SOURCE

Electric power for *Curiosity* and all of its tools comes from a generator called a radioisotope power system. Heat is given off by the natural decay of the rover's supply of plutonium-238, a radioactive metal. The heat is converted into electricity in the rover's generator. The plutonium-238 also provides heat to keep the rover and its instruments from freezing during the frigid Martian nights, when the temperature can drop below -100°F (-73°C).

Earlier generations of Mars rovers used external solar panels to generate electricity. The engineers who built *Curiosity* decided to use the radioisotope system instead because it is more reliable than solar power. Solar panels only work during the day and are sensitive to dust. Solar panels are also large and heavy. The radioisotope system is small and lightweight and can be sealed tightly so it is not affected by dust.

These three images are versions of a single photo taken by *Curiosity*'s mast camera. The image on the left reflects the state in which the photo is initially received on Earth, with no color correcting. The center photo shows scientific color correcting to estimate what the colors would look like on Mars itself. The image at right is an estimate of what the colors would look like under Earth, rather than Martian, lighting.

CHAPTER 2

THE MARTIAN LANDSCAPE

Mars is famous as the red planet of the solar system. In fact, its color is the reason it got its name. The red color reminded ancient Romans of blood, so they named the planet after Mars, their god of war. In photos of Mars taken from the surface by landers, *everything* about Mars is red. The rocks are red, the sand dunes are red—even the sky is salmon pink.

But why is Mars red? The soil on Mars consists of clays that contain large amounts of iron-rich minerals. This iron has combined with oxygen to form iron oxides, a process we think of as rusting. If you have ever seen a rusty piece of iron or steel, you have seen iron oxide, which is reddish. So basically, Mars is red because it is rusting! And most of the oxygen that scientists believe Mars may once have had is trapped in its iron-rich clays.

Martian atmosphere

A typical day on Mars might be beautiful and clear, without a cloud in the bright pink sky. There may be only a few wisps of dust raised by a slight breeze. It might be as warm as 60°F (15°C). A few days later, however, the temperature might plummet to -150°F (-100°C), with brilliant clouds of water crystals appearing in the sky. The following week, a dust storm might blanket the entire planet under an opaque yellow cloud. Changes as dramatic as these can happen all the time on Mars, with the planet experiencing abrupt planetwide swings between dusty and hot and cloudy and cold. These shifts in global climate are driven by three important factors: Mars's thin atmosphere, its elliptical orbit around the sun, and the effects of dust and water ice clouds in the atmosphere.

Temperatures on Mars can change more quickly and intensely than they do on Earth because Mars's atmosphere is one hundred times thinner than that of the earth. The dense atmosphere of our planet acts like a blanket, retaining the heat Earth receives from the sun. In addition, Mars does not have oceans to store up solar heat. Ocean waters absorb heat, releasing it back into the atmosphere slowly. These things help keep Earth's temperature from changing rapidly.

When the sun heats the surface of Mars, the air above grows warmer and rises. Rising warm air, with cold air moving in to replace it, generates wind. Since most of Mars's surface is covered with fine dust particles, even very weak winds can easily stir them up. For this reason, tornado-like dust devils occur during the day when the heated air rises rapidly and becomes turbulent. When the prevailing winds become strong, they can cause violent regional storms.

Winds on Mars can reach surprising speeds. While wind speeds measured at the two *Viking* lander sites in the 1970s were usually a gentle 10 miles (17 km) per hour or less, gusts of up to 30 miles (50 km) per hour were also observed. At the height of a major dust storm on Mars, however, winds may reach hundreds of miles (hundreds of kilometers) an hour.

MARS'S ATMOSPHERE

Mars's atmosphere is thin but still dense enough for clouds to form and for winds to blow across the surface. These winds can raise giant clouds of dust and even form dust devils. The atmosphere of Mars is so full of dust that the sky is pink instead of blue.

The atmosphere of Earth is divided into five layers, but the atmosphere of Mars has only three. The lowest layer, the one nearest the surface, is called the troposphere. Most of the active weather takes place in this region. This is where the atmosphere

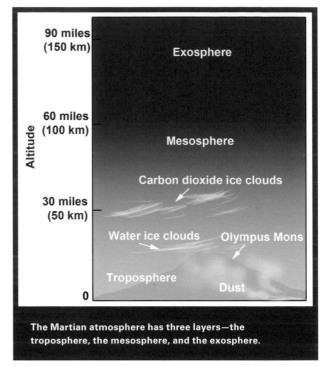

The Martian atmosphere has three layers—the troposphere, the mesosphere, and the exosphere.

is most affected by heat from the sun-warmed surface and airborne dust. Above the troposphere is the mesosphere. It is the coldest part of Mars's atmosphere. The next layer is called the exosphere. From here the atmosphere rapidly fades into the vacuum of space.

MARTIAN CLIMATE AND WEATHER

Weather and climate are often confused. Weather refers to changes in temperatures and precipitation from day to day or week to week. Climate, on the other hand, refers to the average temperatures and precipitation of a large area over a long period of time. To understand the distinction, think of a region with a dry *climate,* such as a desert. It can have rainy *weather* now and again.

The climate on Mars is cold and dry. The average temperature is only -80°F (-60°C). But just because Mars is cold and dry doesn't mean it doesn't have weather. In fact, Mars has a very complex, active weather system. To help scientists study Martian weather, the MSL rover carries a complete weather station. The Rover Environmental Monitoring Station (REMS) measures atmospheric pressure, wind speed and direction, and air temperature and ground temperature, among other things.

REMS

The *Curiosity* rover is equipped with a weather station called the Rover Environmental Monitoring Station, or REMS. This is a package of instruments designed to record air and ground temperature, wind speed and direction, and atmospheric pressure. Information gathered by the REMS enables scientists to better understand how weather on Mars works, especially small-scale local weather. REMS will also enable scientists to determine the likelihood that life might exist beneath the surface, by determining how the atmosphere and the soil of Mars interact.

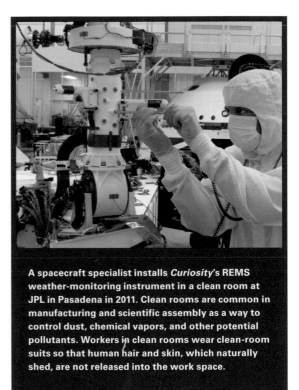

A spacecraft specialist installs *Curiosity*'s REMS weather-monitoring instrument in a clean room at JPL in Pasadena in 2011. Clean rooms are common in manufacturing and scientific assembly as a way to control dust, chemical vapors, and other potential pollutants. Workers in clean rooms wear clean-room suits so that human hair and skin, which naturally shed, are not released into the work space.

Much of Mars's weather is created by the changing seasons. The axis of Mars (an imaginary line around which the planet rotates) is tipped almost the same amount as Earth's (25.19 degrees for Mars, 23.45 degrees for Earth). As on Earth, this axial tilt creates seasons. Mars has seasons almost exactly like our own—spring, summer, winter, and fall. A day on Mars is almost exactly as long as a day on

Earth (24.6 hours for Mars, 23.9 hours for Earth). A Martian day is called a sol. A year on Mars, however, is almost twice as long as an Earth year. Earth takes 365 days to circle the sun, while Mars takes 687 days. For this reason, Mars's seasons are twice as long. When Mars's northern hemisphere is tilted toward the sun, it experiences summer, while the southern hemisphere has winter. Six months later, the northern hemisphere tilts away from the sun and the seasons are reversed.

For Earth, which has an almost perfectly circular orbit, there is little difference between the seasons of the northern and southern hemispheres. Summer in the southern hemisphere is not much hotter than summer in the northern hemisphere. The orbit of Mars, on the other hand, is distinctly elliptical. This means that during its orbit, Mars is not always the same distance from the sun. For example, Mars is closest to the sun during the southern hemisphere's summer. Mars is farthest from the sun when the northern hemisphere is having its summer. This means that summers in the southern hemisphere of Mars tend to be shorter and hotter than summers in the northern hemisphere.

When Mars is nearest the sun,

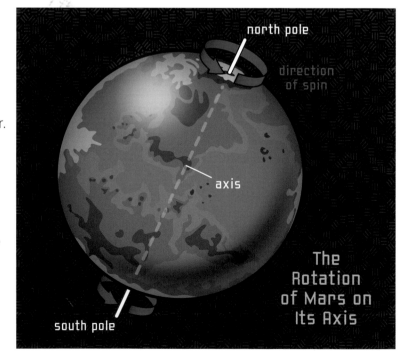

north pole

direction of spin

axis

The Rotation of Mars on Its Axis

south pole

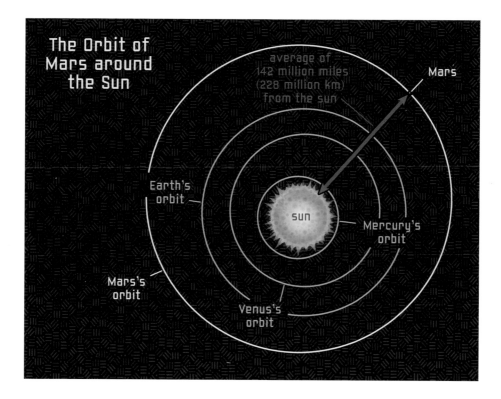

The Orbit of Mars around the Sun

average of 142 million miles (228 million km) from the sun

Mars

Earth's orbit

sun

Mercury's orbit

Mars's orbit

Venus's orbit

the increased solar radiation creates a large temperature difference between the lower and upper parts of the Martian atmosphere. For instance, at ground level, the temperature might be between -135°F (-93°C) and -99°F (-73°C). At an altitude of 50 miles (80 km), the temperature may be as low as -280°F (-173°C). This causes convection to occur, and the clash of warmer and cooler air results in storms. Because Mars is a dry planet, these storms often blanket the planet with dust. The dust absorbs sunlight, further warming the atmosphere.

On the other hand, when Mars is farthest from the sun, the planet experiences fewer temperature differences in its atmosphere. This results in a calmer atmosphere. As a result, Mars has two distinct summer seasons: a warm, dusty southern summer and a cold, dust-free northern summer.

CONVECTION

Convection occurs when there is a difference in temperature between two layers of a gas or liquid. When you make soup in a pan, the soup at the bottom of the pan gets hot before the soup at the top. The hot soup will rise to the surface while the cooler soup sinks to the bottom. A kind of circular motion is created. This motion is called convection and is one way

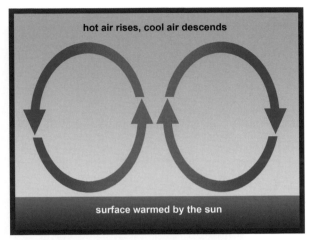

hot air rises, cool air descends

surface warmed by the sun

in which heat can be transferred from one place to another. Convection occurs in the atmosphere of a planet when air is heated by the sun-warmed surface. This air rises while cooler air high in the atmosphere sinks.

OVER HILL, OVER DALE

Astronomers once believed that Mars was a vast, flat desert. They thought it had no high mountains or deep valleys. At best, they thought, there might be only low rolling hills and sand dunes. The first images of Mars sent back to Earth by spacecraft changed all that. We now know that Mars has the largest known mountains in the solar system and the biggest canyon.

The greatest of the Martian mountains is Olympus Mons (Latin for Mount Olympus), which was named after the home of the gods in Greek mythology. Olympus Mons is a giant volcano that towers 13 miles (21 km) above the surrounding landscape; that's nearly three times taller than Earth's Mount Everest! The volcanic mountain is so high that the summit rises above most of Mars's atmosphere. The base of Olympus Mons would entirely cover the state of Missouri. It sits among three other giant volcanoes.

Just to the east of the great volcanoes of Mars is a system of canyons called Valles Marineris, or Mariner Valleys. They were named after the *Mariner 9* spacecraft that discovered them in 1971. It is the greatest known canyon in the solar system. Earth's Grand Canyon stretches across the northwestern corner of Arizona for 280 miles (450 km). By contrast, Valles Marineris would stretch across the entire United States, from the Atlantic Ocean to the Pacific Ocean—more than 2,500 miles (4,000 km). With a depth of up to 3 to 4 miles (5 to 7 km), some of its valleys are about four times deeper than the Grand Canyon.

Mars has vast deserts covered with sand dunes, just like the deserts on Earth. The sand dunes are created by wind blowing dust and sand. The red planet also has thousands of craters. These were created by the impact of meteoroids and asteroids over the course of millions of years. Gale Crater is one of these.

HEADING FOR THE POLES

Another distinctive feature of Mars is its polar caps. They were first noticed hundreds of years ago, when humans first turned telescopes toward the planet. The Martian poles are bright, white patches that stand out

Mars's Valles Marineris (Mariner Valleys) is the largest known canyon system in the solar system. It is visible from space and far surpasses Earth's Grand Canyon in length and depth.

Winds blowing off the ice on Mars's north pole have pushed sand into dunes. This panoramic scene of the pole combines images taken between December 2002 and February 2005 by an imaging instrument on NASA's *Mars Odyssey*.

distinctly against the reddish planet. The polar caps were among the first features to be observed on Mars, and astronomers were certain from the very beginning that they were either frozen water or frozen carbon dioxide (also known as dry ice), or a combination of both. From modern space missions to Mars, we know that each polar cap has a permanent layer of water ice that is covered by a larger, seasonal cap of carbon dioxide ice. The temperatures at the poles can drop to as low as -238°F (-150°C).

The two caps are not identical. The northern polar cap is the larger of the two. With a 600-mile (965 km) diameter, it is almost three times larger than the southern cap, which has a diameter of 220 miles (350 km). The southern seasonal cap, which is smaller and brighter than the northern cap, forms when the atmosphere has much less dust in it. The southern polar cap contains more water ice, too.

RIVERBEDS AND ANCIENT LAKES

Among the most distinct features of Mars are the hundreds of channels that meander across its surface. These were once the beds of rivers and streams. Orbiting spacecraft and surface rovers have also detected the shorelines of large lakes, seas even, that once existed on Mars. Today, there are few signs of water on the surface of Mars. Where did all that water go? In September 2013, the *Curiosity* rover discovered part of the answer. It found huge amounts of water locked in the soil of Mars. There might be as much as 250 gallons (946 liters) of water in the amount of soil it would take to fill the average room in a house. This is encouraging news for NASA as it plans future manned missions to the red planet.

Brazilian-born artist Henrique Alvim Corrêa created this illustration for a 1906 edition of H. G. Wells's *War of the Worlds* to show Martian tripods advancing against humans.

CHAPTER 3

LIFE ON MARS

Mars has always held a special fascination for humans, in large part because it is the most Earth-like of all the planets. It has a day almost exactly as long as Earth's, regular seasons, an atmosphere, polar ice caps, volcanoes, and many other familiar features. It is a very cold world, and the air is one hundred times thinner than on Earth, but if you were to visit Mars, it would look a lot like home.

Venus is much more like Earth's twin in size and composition, but it is covered with sulfuric acid clouds, and its scorching temperatures rise as high as 891°F (477°C). Mercury is airless and three times closer to the sun than Earth. Jupiter, Saturn, Uranus, and Neptune are all giant, frigid spheres of poisonous gases. In comparison to these other worlds in the solar system, Mars seems downright friendly. So friendly that scientists think it may once have been home to some form of life—and may one day support human life.

MARS IN THE IMAGINATION

In the late nineteenth century, an amateur American astronomer and author named Percival Lowell wrote several books claiming that Mars was teeming with life. Very few astronomers took Lowell's ideas seriously, but the public embraced them enthusiastically. Mars fever swept the world. Everything from novels and magazine articles to plays and fairground rides were inspired by the idea that there might be life on Mars.

One notable English author who was impressed by Lowell's theory was H. G. Wells. He was inspired to write the classic science fiction novel *The War of the Worlds* (1898). An American author, Edgar Rice Burroughs (author of the Tarzan series), wrote fabulous

English writer H. G. Wells at his desk in 1940. Among Wells's most famous science fiction works are *The Time Machine* (1895), *The Invisible Man* (1897), and *The War of the Worlds* (1898).

adventures set on a Lowellian Mars inhabited by giant, four-armed, green Martian warriors and beautiful red princesses. His books inspired the motion picture *John Carter* (2012), starring Taylor Kitsch as John Carter and Lynn Collins as the princess he loves. Ray Bradbury, who wrote such classics as *The Martian Chronicles* (1950), speculated in his fiction about what it might feel like to live on Mars.

Mars is still a popular subject for science fiction. For example, Kim Stanley Robinson's famous trilogy—*Red Mars* (1993), *Blue Mars* (1994), and *Green Mars* (1996)—describes the exploration and future colonization of the planet with scrupulous attention to scientific detail and realism. *Mission to Mars* (2000) is a film about an expedition to Mars and a mystery that is discovered there. *Red Planet* (2000) is another Mars-themed science fiction film that focuses on a story about terraforming Mars for human colonization. *Stranded* (2001) tells about a mission to Mars where everything goes wrong and the crew has to struggle to survive on the hostile world.

ON ANCIENT MARS

Scientists know that Mars has all the ingredients for life. Or at least it once did, millions of years ago. The planet was warmer then and had liquid water. It had all the same elements, minerals, and chemical compounds as Earth did when life first formed here. Also like early Earth, Mars had energy from volcanoes and the sun. Billions of years ago, Mars also had vast lakes and maybe even oceans. These seas were probably a mix of minerals and elements washed from the land by rain and meteor impacts. The water also probably had vast amounts of dissolved carbon dioxide.

Carbon dioxide (CO_2) is a combination of carbon and oxygen. Carbon has many special properties. Among them is the ability to form large, complex molecules in combination with a great many other elements, such as hydrogen, nitrogen, and oxygen. Carbon-based molecules can split into two identical halves. When they do this, they reproduce themselves. This ability to reproduce is the foundation of life.

Scientists know that the billions of different complex molecules that formed in Earth's ancient oceans were the building blocks from which more complex life forms developed. For this reason, scientists wonder if complex, self-reproducing molecules might have also formed in the carbon-rich chemical waters of early Martian seas.

IS MARS HABITABLE?

The MSL mission has one overarching objective: to determine if Mars is habitable. To find out, the mission focuses on four main areas of study. They are to examine the Martian geological landscape; to study water and carbon dioxide and other atmospheric elements on Mars; to search for key chemical compounds (gases and minerals) that could support life; and to research Martian radiation levels.

To accomplish all this, _Curiosity_ is analyzing samples taken from the soil and rocks on Mars. The laboratory built into the rover then looks for organic (carbon) compounds, a potential telltale sign of life.

To obtain samples, *Curiosity* uses the drill on its SAM instrument. The powdered rock created by the drill is transferred to the CheMin laboratory inside the rover. There the rock is heated to 2,000°F (1,093°C). This turns any organic compounds and other substances into gases that can be identified by the CheMin instruments.

Soil Samples

In February 2013, *Curiosity* drilled its first hole into a rock. It was only 2.5 inches (6.3 centimeters) deep and 0.6 inches (1.5 cm) wide. The drilling took place in a low area called Yellowknife Bay, not far from where *Curiosity* landed. The bay may have been filled with water millions of years ago. It's exactly the kind of place where organic materials might have been deposited when Mars was a wetter and warmer planet. *Curiosity*'s operators chose a flat-surfaced rock for the first attempt to drill a hole. Since then, *Curiosity* has taken samples from several other sites in the area.

After testing the samples, CheMin has discovered the presence of water, carbon dioxide, oxygen, sulfur dioxide, and hydrogen sulfide and that the rock itself is a kind of clay. Since rocks and soil like this can only form in the presence of flowing water, they are an important clue suggesting that water once flowed freely on Mars.

The earlier Mars exploration rovers had also found evidence for an ancient wet environment. That water, however, would have been far too acidic to support life, and scientists

Curiosity's drill produced this hole in a Martian rock that scientists named John Klein. The drill's bit transported powdered rock from John Klein up into the drill for later chemical analysis.

were skeptical about the possibility of life evolving on Mars. But *Curiosity* has found that the water at Yellowknife Bay would have been just right. In fact, the neutral pH levels (the balance of acidity and alkalinity) and low salt content would have actually encouraged life to evolve and flourish. John Grotzinger, project scientist for the *Curiosity* mission, says the water would have been "so benign and supportive of life that if a human had been on the planet back then, they could drink it."

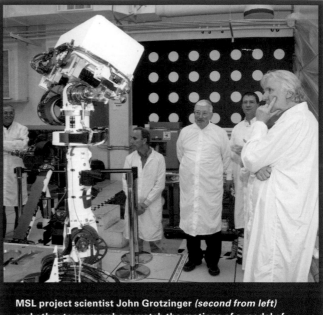

MSL project scientist John Grotzinger *(second from left)* and other team members watch the motions of a model of *Curiosity*'s camera mast prior to mission launch. Film director James Cameron *(far right)* was also part of the mission's camera team.

Taking a Sniff

After *Curiosity* landed, it took a sniff of Mars's atmosphere. *Curiosity*'s readings show that the atmosphere of Mars is made of 96 percent carbon dioxide and small amounts of argon, nitrogen, oxygen, and carbon monoxide. The planet's extreme cold and lack of air pressure and oxygen mean it would be impossible for humans to walk around on the surface of Mars without the protection of space suits.

Curiosity has also been looking for methane in the Martian atmosphere. Methane is an organic gas (a gas that contains carbon) that is often a byproduct of living organisms. Methane can also come from nonbiological sources such as volcanoes. So far, *Curiosity* has failed to discover any methane on Mars.

Radiation Studies

Measuring the amount of solar radiation that reaches the surface of Mars is an important step in determining whether people could live on Mars. On Earth our dense atmosphere acts like a shield, protecting us from dangerous radiation from the sun. Earth's magnetic field also acts as a barrier. But Mars has a thin atmosphere and a very weak magnetic field. So far, *Curiosity*'s measurements show the levels of radiation to be higher than Earth's, yet similar to what astronauts experience at the International Space Station. With these early findings, NASA scientists think that astronauts could potentially endure a round-trip mission to Mars without being exposed to dangerous levels of radiation.

WeT MaRS

As part of the mission to determine whether Mars is habitable, NASA scientists are focusing on learning even more about the history of water on the red planet. When astronomers and other scientists of the 1970s were first able to determine that ancient Mars not only had water but vast amounts of it, they were astonished. Mars is a small planet with a very thin atmosphere. The rate at which water evaporates (turns into a gas) depends on the pressure of the air above it. The lower the pressure, the faster water will evaporate. The very low air pressure on Mars means that it would be nearly impossible for liquid water to exist on the surface: it would almost immediately turn into a gas. The water molecules would eventually disappear into space, lost forever. This is what scientists once believed happened to Mars. Yet large channels, each of which could have been formed only by the massive release of water over a short period of time, scar four regions on Mars: Chryse Planitia, Elysium Planitia, the eastern Hellas Planitia basin, and the Amazonis Planitia. Several of these channels drain into the planet's northern plains. From this, some scientists theorize that an ancient ocean may once have covered most of Mars's northern hemisphere.

ALH84001

ALH84001,0

Curiosity's discovery of water in the soil of Mars was one more piece of evidence among many that Mars was once a wet planet. Another exciting proof of water on ancient Mars appeared in 1984, when scientists exploring Antarctica found a meteorite. It turned out to be a special, very rare type of meteorite that comes from Mars. They called it ALH84001 *(right)*. The 5-pound (2 kg) chunk of Mars collided with Earth about 13,000 years ago. Scientists were able to determine that the meteorite was at least 4 billion years old—much older than Martian meteorites previously discovered on Earth.

Martian meteorites all contain traces of gases and other elements that resemble conditions on the red planet at the time the meteorites were formed. When ALH84001 launched, liquid water was everywhere on the surface of Mars. For this reason, scientists reasoned that the meteorite might contain evidence of ancient life on Mars. In examining the meteorite, scientists found orange carbonate globules that resembled the deposits of limestone found in caves on Earth. Limestone can form only in the presence of liquid water. This was a very encouraging sign.

Scientists then discovered that the globules contained traces of organic compounds as well as magnetite and iron sulfide. These are rarely found in the presence of carbonates unless they are produced by organic processes, such as the metabolism (the process by which an organism uses energy) of bacteria. Additionally, the globules were covered with microscopic wormlike shapes that resembled fossil bacteria.

Many scientists at the time doubted that these were signs of ancient Martian life. They gave examples of ways in which these materials could have been created by nonliving processes. Some scientists also believe that samples such as these may have been contaminated by life on Earth in the thousands of years before the meteorites were discovered. But most scientists of the twenty-first century believe that ALH84001 does indeed contain signs of ancient Martian life.

Other evidence suggests that ancient Mars had flowing water. The southern highlands are crisscrossed by networks of valleys that appear to have been formed by water. And many craters are surrounded by a ring of splattered debris, like that around a stone dropped in soft mud.

Mars missions have also discovered evidence of flooding. Features carved into the Martian landscape downstream in the Martian channels, for example, resemble those

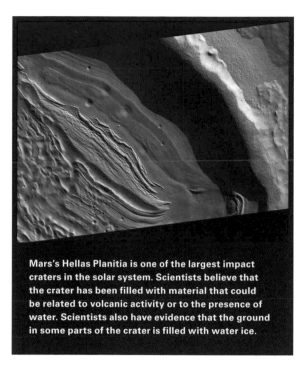

Mars's Hellas Planitia is one of the largest impact craters in the solar system. Scientists believe that the crater has been filled with material that could be related to volcanic activity or to the presence of water. Scientists also have evidence that the ground in some parts of the crater is filled with water ice.

left by ancient flooding on Earth in the state of Washington. Some of the Martian floods were one hundred times larger than the ones in Washington! Some channels on Mars that were created by flowing water, such as those to the east of the Valles Marineris, seem to have formed when an ice dam suddenly collapsed. But others emerge from regions where the ground seems to have collapsed, leaving a chaotic jumble of large blocks of rock. Earth has similar areas of chaotic terrain in Siberia that formed when a layer of underground ice melted suddenly, causing the rock above to fracture and collapse. On Earth this melting was almost always caused by climate changes. On Mars the ice may have been melted by similar climate changes or by the heat of a nearby asteroid impact.

Many scientists estimate that any liquid water on Mars must have existed on the surface before 3.8 billion years ago. Scientists estimate the age of Martian features by a process called crater counting.

GALE CRATER

Within forty days of landing on Mars, *Curiosity* discovered deep channels that appear to have been carved into the sides of Mount Sharp—the mountain in Gale Crater where the rover landed—as well as into the walls of the crater. The channels are evidence of an ancient streambed filled with gravel. The gravel has been cemented together in a solid mass called a conglomerate. The pebbles range in size from grains of sand to golf balls.

The discovery of the conglomerate was almost accidental. The sky crane's rocket engines blasted away dust and dirt from the surface during the landing of the rover, exposing a small outcropping of conglomerate. Scientists directed the rover to look for more and quickly found another outcropping.

The outcropping looks like a section of broken sidewalk. But it's really a section of an ancient tilted streambed, the layers of which scientists can observe.

This rocky outcrop on Mars, called Link, shows rounded gravel fragments as well as groups of smaller rocks cemented together in a mass known as conglomerate. These characteristics are typical of rock that has been transported and shaped by water.

The size and shape of the rocks in the streambeds tell scientists they were transported by water. They are too big to have been carried by wind. The rounded shape of most of the pebbles also shows that the stones were carried by the water for a long distance, smoothed as they ground against each other. Because of the rocks' erosion, scientists know that the stream must have flowed for many years and that the water flowed at about 3 feet (0.9 m) per second. The stream was likely between ankle and hip deep. This discovery adds more important evidence to support the theory of a wet past on Mars.

This is based on the idea that the older the surface of a moon or planet is, the more craters it will have. Additionally, if a crater is on top of a channel, scientists know that the channel is older than the crater. If another crater is on top of *that* crater, then the channel is older than both of them. A close examination of the craters on Mars shows pretty clearly that the most ancient surfaces on Mars—where images show most of the river channels and valley systems indicative of flowing water—must date from very early Mars, more than about 3 billion years ago. *Curiosity's* SAM package of instruments proved that water had not only once existed on Mars, but also existed in large quantities. Scientists came to this conclusion after the SAM discovered that present-day Martian soil is as much as 2 percent water. Mars must once have had a great deal of water on its surface for this much to remain today.

This water must have been there for quite a long time, too, since it would have taken millions of years for many of the water-created features to have formed. But the atmosphere on present-day Mars is too cold and thin to support liquid water on the surface for long and for water ice to form. All of this evidence—ancient riverbeds, deposits of underground ice, water in the soil—suggests that the Mars of 3.8 billion years ago was much warmer and wetter than it is today. If any form of life evolved on Mars, it must have been when all the ingredients—liquid water, warmth, and the necessary chemicals and minerals—were available at the same time.

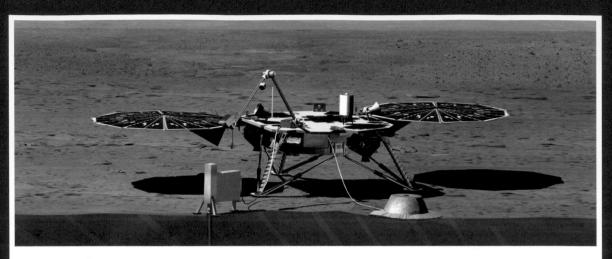

This is an artist's rendering of the *InSight* lander. *InSight* stands for "Interior Exploration using Seismic Investigations, Geodesy and Heat Transport." It is a future space mission to Mars in which JPL, Lockheed Martin Space Systems, the French and German space agencies, and NASA join forces to explore and learn more about the structure of the interior of Mars.

CHAPTER 4
THE FUTURE OF MARS – – – ┘

Mars is already one of the most-explored planets in the solar system, and NASA is planning more probes for the near future. The recent discoveries made by the *Mars Global Surveyor* and the MSL mission—especially the discovery of evidence of large amounts of water on Mars—have spurred more interest in the planet than ever.

The first among the next generation of Mars missions is NASA's Mars Atmosphere and Volatile Evolution Mission (MAVEN) probe. Set to launch in November 2013, its goal is to orbit Mars to study the planet's atmosphere. Scientists hope it will help them understand how Mars lost so much of its atmosphere—and water—to space.

The success of *Curiosity* has led NASA to plan another, similar mission to Mars. Called *InSight*, the mission will launch in 2016. In addition to tools similar to those carried by *Curiosity,* the *InSight* lander will have a seismometer. This instrument will allow scientists to study the interior structure of Mars. The lander will also use a robotic probe to drill as far as 16 feet (5 m) deep into the Martian topsoil. An instrument on the end of the probe will measure how much heat is coming from the interior of Mars.

All of the planets in the solar system formed from a giant cloud of gas and dust that once circled the sun. This gas and dust eventually formed into clumps, which accumulated into even bigger clumps. These became the planets. As the planets grew larger, they became very hot inside. The center of our planet, Earth, is still molten. It is this heat that powers the movement of our continents. Learning the temperature of the interior of Mars will help scientists better understand the history of Mars and how active it may still be in the twenty-first century.

A great many more probes are planned for the near future. These include NASA's scout missions, which will deploy a number of small robotic landers and aircraft and balloons that will range all over the planet. An international mission headed by NASA and the ESA plans to launch the first Mars sample return mission (MSR). The MSR probe will bring the first samples of rocks and soil from the Martian surface back to Earth.

The Indian Space Research Organization (ISRO) hopes to launch its first satellite—named *Mangalyaan*—into orbit around Mars in the near future. The craft's name comes from *Mangala*, the ancient Sanskrit name for Mars.

Other nations have plans to explore Mars. India hopes to launch its *Mangalyaan* spacecraft in 2013. It will orbit Mars, gathering information about the planet. Its main goal, however, is to test India's technology and ability to successfully carry through such a mission. The European

Space Agency and the Russian Federal Space Agency may launch an orbiter and a lander toward Mars in 2018. They will search for past and present signs of life on the planet. Russia is working on a program called Mars-Grunt (*grunt* is the Russian word for "ground"). If successful, the mission would gather samples on Mars and return them to Earth. These and many other missions to Mars may never come to pass, while others will successfully make the journey to the mysterious red planet.

MANNED MISSION TO MARS?

The big question is, when will human beings land on Mars? US president Barack Obama thinks it will happen soon. "By the mid-2030s," he said, "I believe we can send humans to orbit Mars and return them safely to Earth. And a landing on Mars will follow. And I expect to be around to see it."

Sending such a mission to Mars would be a complex project—many times more difficult than sending astronauts to the moon. Over the past fifty years, NASA, private aerospace companies, and individual scientists and engineers have all proposed plans for sending humans to the red planet. As many space scientists have pointed out, we have long had the technology and science to enable humans to get to Mars. The only thing missing is the will to do it—and the money. The Apollo program to land humans on the moon in the 1960s cost $20 billion. That's the equivalent of $100 billion in twenty-first-century dollars. NASA estimates it would cost about $11 billion to land astronauts on Mars.

One reason it would cost less to go to Mars than it did to go to the moon is that everything needed for the Apollo missions had to be developed almost from the ground up. We now have almost half a century of advancement and experience to draw upon. All the same, many people question spending so much money to go to Mars when there are many important things to do on Earth. The debate is complex. On the one hand, space programs provide jobs for thousands of people. In addition, the research and development involved in the space program generate new technologies and industries that benefit ordinary people around the world. On the other hand, many Americans do not support the use of tax dollars to fund NASA. They suggest that private companies and individuals—whom they view as more efficient—should instead foot the bill. As a result, NASA's space programs have faced major cuts over recent years, and the future of additional Mars programs will depend on the political will to fund them.

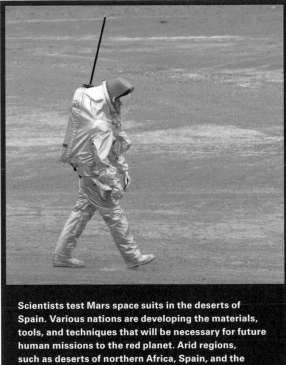

Scientists test Mars space suits in the deserts of Spain. Various nations are developing the materials, tools, and techniques that will be necessary for future human missions to the red planet. Arid regions, such as deserts of northern Africa, Spain, and the southwestern United States, are desirable sites for field tests, since the landscapes there resemble those on Mars.

For now, NASA is hoping to launch a manned mission to Mars in 2030. NASA knows that astronauts on an expedition to Mars would have to be prepared to be away from Earth for more than two and a half years. The mission would consist of a 180-day (6-month) outbound cruise, a 500- to 600-day (20-month) stay on Mars, and another 180-day flight back to Earth. (The exact periods of time would depend on when the mission took place.) One of the reasons for the long stay on Mars is that both Mars and Earth will have moved in their orbits during the long flight to the red planet. The astronauts would have to wait until the two planets return to their nearest position to each other for the shortest flight home.

NASA Spinoffs

Everyone has benefitted from the space program in one way or another. If you have ever watched a movie on a flat-screen TV while texting a friend and eating microwave popcorn, you are using technology developed by NASA. Many of the ways in which NASA technology appears in your daily life are obvious. For example, satellite TV and GPS navigation depend on orbiting satellites to work.

But did you know that the Nike Air shoes you may be wearing were developed from NASA research into shock-absorbing materials? Or that LED lights in your new flashlight came from NASA research? So did the heart pumps that keep patients alive while waiting for

NASA technology led to Nike Air training shoes. A technique called blow rubber molding, used in producing space helmets, was applied to create hollow athletic shoe soles filled with shock-absorbing, interconnected air cells to cushion the foot. Frank Rudy, a former NASA engineer, pitched the idea to Nike, which went on to manufacture the popular shoe.

heart transplants. The solar panels that provide electricity for everything from homes and factories to garden lights were developed by NASA, too, as were home blood pressure monitors and invisible braces for your teeth. Freeze-dried food, memory foam mattresses, and hang gliders all came from the space program. NASA research has also resulted in technologies for safer roads and highways, cleaner air, and cleaner oceans. In fact, NASA has cataloged more than 1,600 new products and technologies that have come from space research!

a TRIP TO MaRS

Over the past fifty years, space scientists and a range of other interested parties have developed many different plans for a trip to Mars. Even the plans for the 2030 trip are likely to undergo changes before it is actually launched. One plan for a trip to Mars would involve three spacecraft for the journey. The first is an unmanned cargo lander. Another is an unoccupied habitat lander, which will go into orbit around Mars. The habitat lander will include an ascent vehicle,

A Rocket for Mars

NASA is developing the most powerful rocket ever built. The Space Launch System (SLS) will be the first rocket in more than forty years designed specifically for space exploration. In addition to carrying important cargo, equipment, and science experiments into space, it will launch the Orion Multi-Purpose Crew Vehicle. This spacecraft will carry up to four astronauts to near-Earth asteroids, the moon, and eventually to the planet Mars.

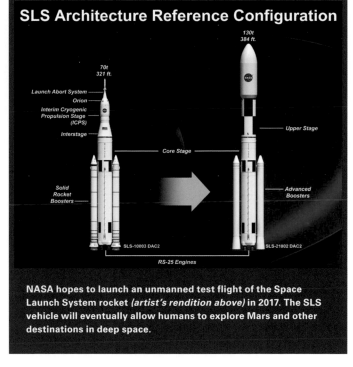

SLS Architecture Reference Configuration

70t
321 ft.

Launch Abort System
Orion
Interim Cryogenic Propulsion Stage (ICPS)
Interstage

Solid Rocket Boosters

SLS-10003 DAC2

Core Stage

RS-25 Engines

130t
384 ft.

Upper Stage

Advanced Boosters

SLS-21002 DAC2

NASA hopes to launch an unmanned test flight of the Space Launch System rocket *(artist's rendition above)* in 2017. The SLS vehicle will eventually allow humans to explore Mars and other destinations in deep space.

The first test launch of the SLS—Exploration Mission 1—will take place in 2017. It will carry an uncrewed Orion spacecraft. If everything works perfectly, Exploration Mission 2— with a crew of four astronauts—will take place in 2021, with hopes for a crewed mission to Mars in the 2030s.

which the astronauts will use to leave Mars once their mission there is complete. The third craft is a crew transfer vehicle (CTV).

The spacecraft will be assembled in space. Parts will be launched from Earth using NASA's giant new Space Launch System (SLS) rocket. Once all the parts are in orbit, astronauts will assemble the final spacecraft. The cargo lander and habitat will be assembled and launched first. It will take a year for them to reach Mars. Once there, the habitat will go into orbit. The cargo lander will land on Mars. When the cargo lander and habitat have successfully reached Mars, the CTV will leave Earth orbit, carrying its crew of astronauts. They will arrive on Mars thirty-two months after the lander and habitat leave Earth.

NASA astronauts work in a weightless environment on the International Space Station, which has been orbiting Earth since 1998. Any human mission to Mars will have to deal with the effects of long-term weightlessness on the human body.

EN ROUTE TO MARS

The astronauts' trip to Mars will take six months. During that time, they will have to deal with weightlessness, radiation, and boredom. Astronauts aboard the International Space Station spend months in the weightless environment of space. During that time, they lose significant amounts of bone mass, which can be dangerous to human health. Prolonged weightlessness causes other medical problems, including vision loss, fatigue, space sickness (resembling motion sickness), and fluid redistribution leading to cold-like symptoms. One way to address these problems would be to rotate the spacecraft to create artificial gravity. But such a spacecraft would be much more complicated and expensive to construct. Instead, scientists are hoping that special exercise programs will help with the problems associated with weightlessness.

Radiation streams through space constantly. Living creatures on Earth are protected from this radiation by Earth's atmosphere and magnetic field. But an astronaut in space does not have this protection. Most astronauts do not stay in space long enough to accumulate a dangerous dosage. But astronauts on a Mars expedition will be spending a year or more in space, plus about eighteen months on Mars itself. The planet does not have a magnetic field and thick atmosphere to protect astronauts from radiation exposure. Scientists believe that the exposure to radiation would increase an astronaut's chance of developing cancer over the following thirty years by a few percentage points.

A greater radiation risk for the astronauts would come from a solar flare, which could occur any time during the Mars expedition. Solar flares are sudden bursts of high-intensity energy from the sun. They occur unpredictably, so there is no way of telling whether one will happen during the flight to and from Mars. During a solar flare, an astronaut could receive in just a few seconds more than fifty times the amount of radiation she might have received during a full year in space.

Radiation from a solar flare could be blocked by special shielding. For example, scientists know that a layer of water just 4 inches (10 cm) thick would reduce the solar energy to a safe level. If all the water needed for the round trip to Mars were to be stored in the walls of a special cabin in the CTV, this could potentially function as a kind of storm shelter to which the astronauts could flee in case of a solar flare.

Boredom is a psychological risk for men and women sealed in a small space for long periods of time. To head off boredom, astronauts would be tasked with science experiments to perform, observations and data to record, medical tests to take, exercise regimens, and general housekeeping. They would also have plenty of entertainment from books, movies, and games.

SETTING FOOT ON MARS

Once the CTV arrives in orbit around Mars, it will meet up with the habitat lander. The astronauts will transfer from the CTV to the habitat

Scientists anticipate that the first humans on Mars will live and work in habitats resembling these at the Mars Desert Research Station in Utah. Everything that humans will need to survive on the red planet—including electricity, food, oxygen, and water—will have to be produced, repaired, or replaced on-site.

lander. (The CTV will remain in orbit until the astronauts complete their stay on Mars.) The astronauts will make the descent to Mars, landing near the cargo lander. The astronauts will stay on Mars for five hundred to six hundred days, exploring and gathering specimens. To do this, the astronauts will likely have a pressurized rover to travel long distances from the main habitat, or base, on Mars. They will also conduct experiments, many of which will investigate human survival on Mars.

While on Mars, the astronauts would live in the rocket-like habitat lander. It would be attached to the pressurized rover on one side and a greenhouse for plant experiments on the other. Astronauts would be equipped with supplies of oxygen and food, power and water, medical and personal hygiene facilities, a laboratory, and communications equipment.

At the end of their stay, the astronauts will leave Mars in the ascent vehicle. Once back in orbit around Mars, they will rendezvous with the CTV, which will carry them back home to Earth.

LIVING ON MARS

The Mars Society—a private organization devoted to promoting the human exploration of Mars—created a pair of Mars research stations in the early 2000s. They are located in places on Earth that resemble Mars in some way. One is on a barren island in Canada, far to the north of the Arctic Circle. The other is in the desert in southern Utah. While neither of these locations is as cold, dry, and airless as Mars, each is about as close as anyone on Earth can get to a Martian landscape. In these places, the Mars Society has constructed two habitats similar to those that future astronauts might live in. The research stations also include greenhouses, observatories, and dune buggies that stand in for rovers.

Geologist Melissa Battler is the commander of Crew 125 EuroMoonMars B mission at the Mars Desert Research Station in Utah. The mission is investigating the feasibility of humans living on Mars. At the station, mission crews—including students, scientists, and Mars enthusiasts—live at the station in two-week rotations, with limited supplies of basic necessities. They wear simulated space suits and carry air supply packs at all times.

Researchers live in the habitats for up to two weeks at a time. The goal of the Canadian station is to eventually have a crew remain there an entire year. During their stay, the crew wears space suits when going outside. They can only communicate with each other and with the habitat by radio.

During their stay on "Mars," the station crews must live on their own resources—they cannot obtain any supplies, including food and water, from Earth. They must exist on what they already have in the habitat or find ways to create their own air, water, and food.

The purpose of the Mars research stations is to test the ability of humans to live under Mars-like conditions. They are helping to develop and test the design of Mars habitats, as well as the skills, techniques, and tools that will be needed for the continued exploration of Mars.

This illustration offers one vision of a terraformed Mars, in which humans transform the red planet into an environment that resembles the life-sustaining conditions of Earth.

Every twenty-six months after that, another three spacecraft will make the journey to Mars, eventually building up the foundation for a permanent human settlement. Future missions will include automatic propellant factories, which will manufacture fuel from raw materials found on Mars. If this is a successful method for developing fuel, future missions would not have to carry fuel for the round trip. Other factories will produce oxygen and water, while food will be grown in greenhouses. Soon people will be living on Mars in some comfort.

TERRAFORMING MARS

At some point, human colonists will want to live on the surface of Mars, out in the open like we do on Earth. To do so, humans would have to make Mars into a much more Earth-like planet through a process called terraforming. For example, through terraforming, humans could create a much denser atmosphere on Mars so that liquid water could exist in the open without instantly evaporating. A denser atmosphere would also contain heat from the sun so that Mars would grow warmer.

One way to make the atmosphere on Mars denser would be to increase the amount of carbon dioxide in it. Carbon dioxide is a very heavy gas, heavier than oxygen or nitrogen, so it would not take much to increase the density. Since the Martian polar caps are almost solid carbon dioxide, some scientists have suggested melting them. This would release huge amounts of carbon dioxide into the atmosphere. One way to do this would be to place a giant mirror in orbit around

Mars. It would have to be huge—perhaps as much as 100 miles (175 km) wide. This would not be difficult to do if the mirror were made of very thin plastic coated with a shiny metal. The mirror would reflect sunlight onto one of the polar caps. The increased temperature would melt and release the carbon dioxide there.

It might take as long as fifty years for enough carbon dioxide to be released in this way, however. Even then, the air pressure would only be about one-third of that on the surface of Earth. All the same, this would be more than enough to make Mars warm enough to be habitable.

PROBLEMS TO SOLVE

Terraformers will have to find a way to create reliable sources of both oxygen and liquid water on Mars. By increasing warmth and air pressure on Mars, humans could unlock sources of water by simply scooping up shovelfuls of Martian soil and extracting the water it contains.

Getting oxygen into the atmosphere will be a more difficult challenge. Scientists know that large amounts of oxygen are bound up in minerals in the Martian soil, but it would take a lot of energy to release. They also know that plants thrive in carbon dioxide, producing oxygen as a waste product. Almost all of the oxygen in Earth's atmosphere comes from plants. Once humans are able to sufficiently warm Mars, they could cultivate plants, allowing them to spread as fast as they will grow.

In perhaps less than a century after terraforming starts, Mars could become a new world, a second Earth. Humans on Mars would admire clouds floating in a dark blue sky, seas, lakes and rivers, and once-barren deserts covered with forests and green fields. Can you imagine such a future?

SOURCE NOTES

7   "NASA Selects Student's Entry as New Mars Rover Name," NASA, May 27, 2009, http://www.nasa.gov/mission_pages/msl/msl-20090527_prt.htm.

7   Ibid.

19 John Grotzinger, in Nicolle Willett, "Consumable Water on Mars Confirmed by *Opportunity* and *Curiosity*," *Mars Society*, no. 18, June 9, 2013, http://education2.marssociety.org/author/nicolew/page/2/.

34 Ibid.

42 Associated Press, "Obama to NASA: We'll Go to Mars in My Lifetime," Newsmax, April 15, 2010, http://www.newsmax.com/Newsfront/barack-Obama-Space-program/2010/04/15/id/355854.

GLOSSARY

atmosphere: the mixture of gases that surrounds a planet

carbon dioxide: a molecule made of one atom of carbon and two atoms of oxygen. On Earth carbon dioxide is usually found as a gas. On Mars it is found as a gas in the atmosphere and frozen as an ice at the poles.

clay: a type of soil composed of water, silicates, and other minerals

climate: the average condition of the weather in a region

convection: the circulation of heat in a gas or liquid

crater: a circular pit or basin created by the impact of a meteorite

crater counting: a method of estimating the age of a planet's surface based on the idea that impact craters accumulate at a constant rate

European Space Agency (ESA): a European agency created in 1975 for the exploration of space. The largest financial contributors from among the ESA's twenty member nations are France, Germany, Italy, and the United Kingdom.

habitat: a shelter that allows humans to safely live in a hostile environment, such as that on Mars

hydrogen: the simplest and most abundant of the elements

inert gas: a gas that does not react with other elements

International Space Station (ISS): a large artificial Earth satellite, inhabited by a crew of astronauts and scientists. The ISS was launched in 1998.

lander: a robotic or piloted spacecraft designed to land on another planet

Mars Science Laboratory (MSL): the name of a mission to Mars launched in 2011, inclusive of the cruise stage (to propel the spacecraft to Mars); the entry, descent, and landing system; and the *Curiosity* rover

meteorite: a mass of stone or metal that has fallen onto a planet from space

molecule: a combination of two or more atoms

National Aeronautics and Space Administration (NASA): the agency of the US government responsible for the civilian space program

orbit: the path of an object in space as it moves around another object

organic: living or previously living material that contains carbon

organism: a complex living being

oxygen: a gaseous element necessary for life as we know it

robot: a machine that operates remotely without direct human contact

seismometer: an instrument that measures movements of the ground, such as earthquakes, tremors, and landslides

space sickness: a reaction to weightlessness that is similar to air sickness, car sickness, and other forms of motion sickness

spectroscope: an instrument that can detect the elements that make up a substance by examining the light it emits

terraforming: the technology of changing a planet so that it resembles Earth

thrust: the measure of the push created by a rocket engine

weather: the local state of the atmosphere

Selected Bibliography

Beatty, J. Kelly, Carolyn Collins Petersen, and Andrew Chaikin, eds. *The New Solar System*. Cambridge, MA: Sky Publishing Corp, 1999.

Boyce, Joseph. *The Smithsonian Book of Mars*. Washington, DC: Smithsonian Institution Press, 2002.

Crossley, Robert. "Why Mars?" *Air & Space Smithsonian*, August 2012, 30.

Crossman, Frank. *On to Mars*. Burlington, ON: Apogee Books, 2002.

David, Leonard. "Invaders from Earth." *Air & Space Smithsonian*, August 2012, 26.

Dupas, Alain. *Destination Mars*. London: Firefly Books, 2004.

Freed, David. "Emissary." *Air & Space Smithsonian*, August 2012, 18.

Grant, Andrew. "Robo-Geologist Lands on Mars." *Discover*, January/February 2013, 18.

Gross, Heather. "Rover Tracks." *Air & Space Smithsonian*, August 2012, 25.

Hoverstein, Paul. "Mars Mike." *Air & Space Smithsonian*, August 2012, 18.

NASA. "Curiosity Rover: Mission." Accessed June 2012–May 2013. http://mars.jpl.nasa.gov/msl/mission/.

———. "Curiosity Rover: Science." Accessed June 2012–May 2013. http://marsrovers.jpl.nasa.gov/science/.

———. "Curiosity Rover: Technology." Accessed August 2013. http://marsrovers.jpl.nasa.gov/technology/.

———. "Mars Exploration Rovers: Mission." Accessed June 2012–May 2013. http://marsrovers.jpl.nasa.gov/mission/.

Smithsonian. "Mars Journal." *Air & Space Smithsonian*, August 2012, 38.

Wright, Will. "First Neighborhood on Mars." *Air & Space Smithsonian*, August 2012, 28.

Zubrin, Robert, and Christopher McKay. "Technological Requirements for Terraforming Mars." *The Terraforming Information Pages*. Accessed August 16, 2013. http://www.users.globalnet.co.uk/~mfogg/zubrin.htm.

FOR MORE INFORMATION

Books

Aldrin, Buzz. *Mission to Mars*. Washington, DC: National Geographic, 2013.

Bell, Jim. *Mars 3-D*. New York: Sterling Publishing, 2008.

Godwin, Robert. *Mars: The NASA Mission Reports*. Burlington, ON: Apogee Books, 2000.

Hartmann, William K. *Traveler's Guide to Mars*. New York: Workman Publishing, 2003.

Miller, Ron. *The Seven Wonders of the Rocky Planets and Their Moons*. Minneapolis: Twenty-First Century Books, 2011.

Miller, Ron, and William K. Hartmann. *The Grand Tour*. New York: Workman Publishing, 2005.

Pyle, Rod. *Destination Mars*. Amherst, NY: Prometheus Books, 2012.

Rusch, Elizabeth. *The Mighty Mars Rovers: The Incredible Adventures of* Spirit *and* Opportunity. Scientists in the Field series. Boston: Houghton Mifflin Harcourt Books for Young Readers, 2012.

Sheehan, William. *The Planet Mars: A History of Observation and Discovery*. Tucson: University of Arizona Press, 1996.

Sheehan, William, and Stephen James O'Meara. *Mars: The Lure of the Red Planet*. Amherst, NY: Prometheus Books, 2001.

Siy, Alexandra. *Cars on Mars: Roving the Red Planet*. Watertown, MA: Charlesbridge, 2009.

Wiens, Roger. *Red Rover*. New York: Basic Books, 2013.

Zubrin, Robert. *How to Live on Mars*. New York: Three Rivers Press, 2008.

———. *Mars Direct*. New York: Tarcher, 2013.

Great Fiction about Mars

Mars has inspired more writers than any other planet. Here is a selection of some of the best Mars stories written between the late 1800s and the early twenty-first century.

Bear, Greg. *Moving Mars*. New York: Tor Books, 1993.

Benford, Gregory. *The Martian Race*. New York: Aspect, 1999.

Bova, Ben. *Mars*. New York: Bantam, 1992.

Bradbury, Ray. *The Martian Chronicles*. New York: Avon, 1997. First published 1950 by Doubleday.

Burroughs, Edgar Rice. *A Princess of Mars*. New York: Ballantine, 1990. First published 1917 by A. C. McClurg.

Disch, Thomas M. *The Brave Little Toaster Goes to Mars*. New York: Doubleday, 1988.

Hartmann, William K. *Mars Underground*. New York: Tor Books, 1999.

Heinlein, Robert A. *Red Planet*. New York: Ballantine, 1991. First published 1949 by Scribner's.

Robinson, Kim Stanley. *Blue Mars*. New York: Bantam, 1996.

———. *Green Mars*. New York: Bantam, 1994.

———. *Red Mars*. New York: Bantam, 1993.

Wells, H. G. *The War of the Worlds*. New York: Bantam, 1988. First published 1898 by William Heinemann.

Great Films about Mars

Mars and Martians have also inspired many movies, but only a few have treated the exploration of Mars realistically. Here are a few of the best ones.

Conquest of Space. Los Angeles: Paramount, 1955.

Escape from Mars. Vancouver: Credo Entertainment Group, 1999.

Mission to Mars. Burbank, CA: Touchstone Pictures, 2000.

Red Planet. Burbank, CA : Warner Bros, 2000.

Robinson Crusoe on Mars. New York: Aubrey Schenk Productions, 1964.

Stranded. Universal City, CA: Universal, 2001.

Magazines
Astronomy
http://www.astronomy.com
This magazine is aimed at amateur astronomers and is filled with articles and color photos about the planets, the stars, and the galaxies.

Sky & Telescope
http://www.skyandtelescope.com/
For professionals and serious amateurs, this magazine has in-depth articles as well as many excellent photos that will appeal to readers of all ages.

Websites
Ares Education Topics
http://ares.jsc.nasa.gov/ares/education/program/destinationmars.cfm
This site is geared for students and offers good information about NASA's human Mars mission as well as lots of projects and activities.

Mars Exploration Rovers
http://marsrovers.jpl.nasa.gov/home/
The official Mars rover site offers hundreds of photos and videos and the latest news from Mars.

Mars Science Laboratory: Rover
http://mars.jpl.nasa.gov/msl/mission/rover/
The Jet Propulsion Laboratory (JPL) Mars Science Laboratory site provides many photos from Mars along with detailed information about *Curiosity*.

The Mars Society
http://www.marssociety.org
This organization is devoted to promoting the idea of sending humans to Mars in the next decade.

Mars Today
http://www.fourmilab.ch/cgi-bin/uncgi/Yourtel?aim=4&z=1
This site will help you find Mars in the night sky.

NASA—Mars Science Laboratory, the Next Mars Rover
http://www.nasa.gov/mission_pages/msl/index.html
The official NASA Mars Science Laboratory site has many photos and videos as well as the latest news from Mars.

NASA for Students
http://www.nasa.gov/audience/forstudents/index.html
This is a gateway to many NASA sites about the sun and the planets.

Nine Planets
http://www.nineplanets.org
Detailed information about the sun, the planets, and all the moons is available at this site along with photos and useful links to other sites.

Solar System Simulator
http://space.jpl.nasa.gov/
This amazing website allows visitors to travel to all the planets and the moons and to create views of these distant worlds.

Organizations

American Astronomical Society
2000 Florida Ave. NW, Ste. 400
Washington, DC 20009-1231
http://www.aas.org
This is an organization of amateur and professional astronomers.

Association of Lunar and Planetary Observers
PO Box 13456
Springfield, IL 62791-3456
http://alpo-astronomy.org/
This group of amateur and professional astronomers is devoted to the
observation of the moon and the planets.

Astronomical Society of the Pacific
390 Ashton Ave.
San Francisco, CA 94112
http://www.astrosociety.org
This very active organization of amateur and professional astronomers has
members from all over the United States.

The Planetary Society
65 N. Catalina Ave.
Pasadena, CA 91106-2301
http://www.planetary.org
This society is devoted to promoting human exploration of the solar system.

INDEX

ABOUT THE AUTHOR

Hugo Award–winning author and illustrator Ron Miller specializes in books about science, especially space and astronomy. He has written many titles, including *Chasing the Storm: Tornadoes, Meteorology, and Weather Watching; Is the End of the World Near? From Crackpot Predictions to Scientific Scenarios*; and several titles in the Seven Wonders series. A postage stamp he created is currently on board a spaceship headed for Pluto. His original paintings can be found in collections all over the world. Miller lives in Virginia.

PHOTO ACKNOWLEDGMENTS